JUST SHOW UP

JUST SHOW UP

Keys to Meaningful Relationships and Professional Success

FRANK CASTELLI

Charleston, SC
www.PalmettoPublishing.com

Just Show Up

First Edition

Paperback: 978-1-64990-464-5
Hardcover: 978-1-64111-896-5
eBook: 978-1-64111-938-2

TABLE OF CONTENTS

PREFACE

SAINT PAUL, IN his letter to Timothy, said, "I have fought the good fight, I have finished the race, I have kept the faith" (2 Timothy 4:7, New International Version). When I first heard this, and for some time thereafter, I thought that Paul was being quite boastful yet depressed. As I continued in my career, I developed a new and different appreciation of what he was saying. As we become committed and fully engaged in what we do, we tend to become more critical of what we accomplish. It appears that we are never satisfied and are always trying to be better than we were before. I have always been surrounded by people who strive for one more yard on the football field, one more sale at the end of a fiscal year, one step ahead of where we were yesterday. We can lose sight of what we've accomplished while looking ahead to the next best thing.

In recent years, I've had time to reflect on my life, my career, my shortcomings, and my successes. I see those around me learning and growing, and I find myself, yet again, looking for the next best thing. That is what this project is about:

sharing a lifetime of experiences that molded me into the person who I have become. Hopefully, it will allow someone to view their experiences a little differently and help them make sense of what is happening in their lives. This is an account of actual events and reflections that occurred as far back as I can remember. They are a compilation of good things and not-so-good things that helped me make the decisions, both good and bad, that had an effect on my life. Was it all roses and daisies? No. Did I still grow in the garden? Absolutely.

I really believe that at some point in everybody's life they should give back and share all the knowledge and blessings they received. For the most part, when you look at the progression of a lifetime, you realize that it can be broken up into three segments.

Learning and understanding your dependency on others comprises the first segment. As children, we need our parents' nurturing, care, and attention. We attain the age of reason, usually around years seven through nine, and learn right from wrong. When we attend elementary school, we learn the disciplines of attaining knowledge: repetition, studying, and more repetition. In high school, we add the skills of time management and energy management. We must learn to balance schoolwork, friends, extracurricular activities, and rest. After high school, we decide what path we will take to follow our vocations in life. Usually this involves a learning process but not necessarily higher education. Many people will enter a trade as a profession, while others are excited about opportunities in business, medicine, technology, or human services. However, a common theme is that not all eighteen-year-olds really know what they would like to do immediately, and it may take a trial and error period of time before they get on the right path. The key here is that, because we are on the right track, we are now able to move forward. As already mentioned, this segment involves our dependency on others—parents, friends, teachers, mentors. For that reason, we should understand that we are indebted to all the people who helped us come to a realization of what we would like to do and what type of person we would like to become.

The second segment is comprised of the beginning of our journey—once we are on our own. Once we have found our path (with the help of those who helped shape us), we are willing to learn what it takes to be successful. In a perfect world, we are excited about what we might accomplish if we maintain focus and don't stray off of our path. Because of a sense of well-being, we are more willing to share our thoughts, desires, and dreams with others. Some may take the path I chose—choose a spouse, decide to have children, buy a house, invest in a business, and take on added responsibilities. Others may decide to devote themselves solely to a career and moving up the corporate ladder. Others still will volunteer in their communities and thrive off the smiles on the faces they serve. We usually incur debt and tend to make sacrifices and take chances to achieve our dreams. It is during this period of our life that we better understand the values of mastering time management and energy management. People meet many challenges along the way, and they quickly recognize that in overcoming the challenges, we become stronger and wiser. There are heartaches and joys, failures and accomplishments, frustrations and commitments. For these reasons, it becomes imperative to have balance in one's life. It is in working toward that balance that we begin to enter the third segment.

In the third segment of our lives, we begin to realize the fruits of our efforts. If we are lucky enough to be on the right path for us, we continue to move forward in our vocations. Many of us bring down our debt, marvel at the growth of our children, work in leadership roles where we have positive influence on others, and most importantly better understand what is essential in life. Hopefully, all of us can look back at our time on this earth knowing that we made a difference. This is a time for us to give back—not only for the people who helped us get here but also for others who entered our lives and could use our insight, knowledge, understanding, and help. As is stated in the Gospel of Mark, "to whom much is given, much is expected" (Luke 12:48, King James Version). We all have been bestowed numerous blessings, and we all should share what is good and right in the world.

CHAPTER 1

EMBRACE YOUR UNIQUENESS

I WAS BORN on June 13, 1951, in the Bronx, New York City. My mother, Crucifissia, was taken into the hospital because she cut her pinky finger on a broken glass in the sink. Shortly after this incident, likely due to the stress, she went into labor, and I was born a "blue baby" in Westchester Square Hospital. Unfortunately, Mom's stress didn't end there.

In 1951, doctors handled blue babies differently than they do today. I was blue due to lack of oxygen because the umbilical cord was wrapped around my neck. The only thing the hospital could do was put me upside down in the incubator. All my mother could do was pray that I would be all right.

June 13 is the feast day of Saint Anthony. My father's name is Francis Aloysius, and I was supposed to be Francis Aloysius II. However, my mother made a silent novena to Saint Anthony and said that if I survived, I would be Francis Anthony. So here I am, and I was named Francis Anthony Castelli on June 13, 1951. My initials F. A. C. are the sixth, first, and third letters of the alphabet, and these numbers are the numeric representation of my birthdate, June 13 (6/13). I do not believe in coincidences; rather, I believe in destiny. More on that later.

So what's the point? Why did Mom share the story? Although it made for good conversation, what was the lesson to be learned? Mom rarely talked about feelings. She took people and happenings at face value and concluded her own decisions. It took some years for her to let on, but my mom was making a point. She was letting me know that I was unique and that everybody was special in their own way. Mom made a point to make all her children understand their uniqueness and that they, too, were special.

Think of someone you've met in your life who was singularly unique and how that made that person special. I wonder how many times somebody was made fun of or picked on simply because they were different. Imagine Cindy Crawford bearing the brunt of malicious talk because she had a mole near her lip. Think of children asking young Cindy what that mark was on her face. Now think how that little spot, among other qualities, enabled her to become one of the top models in the world. Her birthmark didn't make her famous, but its uniqueness helped her get noticed. Or what about Bill Gates? I'm sure it seemed odd to his friends that he would rather be on a computer than outside playing. But without his unique qualities and devotion to technology, I likely wouldn't be typing this right now.

When I was nine, I met a new friend named Pete. He was very skinny, stood average height, and had a scrawny appearance. He looked like a big wind could knock him down. On top of that, he was pretty shy and so soft-spoken that you had to strain to hear what he was saying. There was not one imposing thing about him. However, he was introduced as a new friend, and we accepted him as such. Everyone who wanted to meet up with us on a daily basis was considered a new friend and part of our sandlot gang—no questions asked.

Pete wanted to play baseball with us. At first, we were reluctant to go full speed with him or even let him go full speed with us; the last thing we wanted to do was get the poor guy hurt. In 1960, if one of your friends got hurt while you were playing and it could have been avoided, you were in big trouble. There was an unspoken code among us men (boys) that friends looked out for friends. We all watched out for each other. Nevertheless, Pete played every day with us on a makeshift field. He played almost every position but really wanted to be a pitcher. Again, we thought twice about this, but since I was the catcher, I agreed to it.

I got the team to agree for Pete to pitch. For some time, he got shellacked. Almost every day, Pete wanted to pitch, and if you were on his pickup team, you didn't want him to play that position. You were going to lose. However, I could tell that Pete knew he had no choice but to embrace his stature. Instead of getting discouraged, he threw himself into pitching, day after day, game after game.

In 1964, four years later, I caught for him in an all-star Babe Ruth game. I had not seen him for a couple of years and asked this now six-foot, ninety-pound, curly blond–haired teammate what pitches he had and what signs he wanted me to use. One finger was for the curve, two fingers were for the screwball, three fingers were for the slider, and four fingers were for the knuckleball. No fastball. And he had all of this arsenal at the age of thirteen. Because it was an all-star game and we were all from different teams, he was only allowed to pitch three innings. Nine batters later, only one batter was able to foul off one pitch. Nine straight strikeouts. How is that for being uniquely different? He used his size and stature to hone his talent. He became the best because of his unique skills.

Uniqueness comes in many sizes, shapes, and personal traits. It can be something physical, like Pete; or it can be intellectual, like a musical prodigy; or it can be emotional, like an empath. The point is if we really want to find the best in each other, look for the differences, the uniqueness, the attributes that set us apart. Recognize that it is in these differences that we are each special, and by treating others special because of their differences, they tend to want to learn more about us. We are all complex, multifaceted pieces of a jigsaw puzzle, and by being aware and looking for the differences, we find not twins but complements, which ultimately make up for our deficiencies. By the way, Pete used all of his training from baseball and funneled that into golf. He became a golf pro, and I went to him for a lesson in 1973. He told me that I had a baseball swing and that he could take that swing and modify it for golf because he had already done it himself. I have the same swing on the golf course today. I guess embracing his uniqueness as a kid worked out—he didn't charge me for the lesson.

CHAPTER 2

A GOOD FOUNDATION

FROM THE MINUTE I was born, with the help of others, I had to overcome adversity. From my first minutes on earth, I had to conquer learning how to breathe. My mother got pregnant with her second son, Richard, six weeks after I was born. Seven months later, a very small, premature, fragile baby was born.

Needless to say, Richard needed a lot of care and attention. I was less than ten months old, and my baby brother needed all the attention that was available. To this day, my mother reminds our entire family that she didn't know how I made it, and if it wasn't for my great-grandmother literally holding me for most of the day, I probably would not be where I am today. I was fiercely colicky, and my grandmother, Nauna Petranella, rocked me in her rocking chair for hours. In addition, Nauna spoke no English and spoke to me in Italian. Everyone wondered whether my first comprehendible words would be in English or Italian. You guessed right if you said both. The first words I said were "Mama" and "Nonna," acceptable in both languages.

In the early 1950s, it was generally accepted that the firstborn male in an Italian family was the leader of the pack. I was not only the firstborn male of my family but also the firstborn male of twenty-four direct cousins. My parents, grandmother, and aunts and uncles made it very clear that I was responsible for the actions of others.

The funny thing about this responsibility was that my birthright was never questioned by my siblings or my cousins. They were told to listen to Francis, and if things went awry, I was held responsible and accountable. Sure, when we were all teenagers, I received pushback, especially when I was telling cousins that they couldn't hang out in shady places or keep company with unsavory people. For the most part, I had the backing of my parents and their parents. I guess I did okay—they still call me for advice to this day.

I was taught three general principles by my father to help me in leading this crazy, loud Italian family: (1) do what's right; (2) do the best you can; (3) follow the Golden Rule—that is, treat others like you would like to be treated. Anytime there was an issue to be discussed, my father would sit us down and ask those three questions. Did we do what was right? For our vehemently Catholic family, this was pretty basic. There are the Ten Commandments and the Eight Beatitudes. These are your reference points. If you didn't keep them, you didn't do what was right. Did we do the best we could? We, as humans, make mistakes, and there is always room for improvement. Rarely did we say that we did the best we could. However, we often said that, at the time, we thought we did so, but knowing what we know now, we would have acted differently. This shows a lesson learned and maturity. Finally, did we treat others like we would have liked to have been treated? Here, we learn how to deal with empathy, sensitivity, and concern for others.

That's it! Those are the foundations on which our families were built. Each and every night, we sat at the dinner table and discussed the events of our day. We came with clean hands and a clean shirt, and for the most part, we finished with a clean heart. You did not miss dinner for a game, a concert, or any other extracurricular event. Dinner was a time of appreciation and conversation—it was considered sacred. Every day, something good and something not so good would happen. But we knew that we could come together every night to discuss it as a family.

Imagine how different our world could be if we spent time having conversations with the ones we love most, reflecting on their family values and building on their family foundation. My parents worked very hard at making sure that when their children put their heads on their pillows, they went to sleep with little or no strife or conflict. Rather, we went knowing that anything could be fixed or forgiven and that a new day brought hope and opportunity.

CHAPTER 3

DEFINING MOMENTS

UPBRINGING, EDUCATION, FAMILY life, and values all take part in who we become. However, each of us have very specific examples of events that took place in our lives that have a tremendous effect on our belief system. Allow me to give you a couple of examples in my life.

It was the summer of 1961. It was a clear, sunny day, and I had just finished my chores—yes, we had chores, and no, we did not get an allowance for doing them. My mother decided to go shopping, and my brothers, Richard and Michael, went with her. At the time, I had just turned eleven years old. My dad had a BB gun in his closet, and we had a small stretch of woods in our backyard. By this time, we had moved from the Bronx into a bedroom community approximately fifty miles north of New York City.

I decided to experiment with the BB gun. As I walked into the woods, I noticed a small, yellowish bird perched on the limb of a tree. Carefully, I aimed the air gun at the bird, took a breath, and pulled the trigger. To my immediate excitement, the bird fell from the tree to the ground. I ran over to see what I had done. As I looked at this small, beautiful, and innocent creature, its breast was pounding hard, and in moments, I saw the life of this bird leave its body. Within seconds, I began to weep uncontrollably. My elation at shooting the little creature turned immediately to despair. What right did I have to take the life of that bird? How could I have been so callous as to not think of what could have happened, what that really meant? I was mentally and emotionally shaken, and I did not know how to handle it.

I went inside the house, put the BB gun back into the closet, and sat in silence in our living room. What was a peaceful, sunny day had been ruined by my actions. When my mother returned from the store, she knew there was something wrong. Sometimes you just couldn't wait for the dinner table to sort out the day's events. When she asked, I couldn't hide my shame and recounted the entire story. She listened intently as I stammered and tried to get through my tale of woe. When I was finished, I knew I was in big trouble.

Yes, I was scolded, and yes, I was told not to use the air gun without my father. But more importantly, my mother asked me how I was going to hold myself accountable. I decided then and there that I would never ever take the life of a living creature again, and I didn't. I am not a hunter, I do not believe in the death penalty, and I hold all life as precious from God. I do not condone euthanasia or abortion. All of this was over one specific incident—a defining moment.

Much later on, I was faced with another defining moment. By this time, I was married, had children, and had a position I started out loving. But as time went on, I became the target of a successor to my previous supervisor and mentor. My new boss did not have the same feelings of admiration and esteem for my mentor as I did. Every day it was abundantly clear that my new boss not only didn't like me but tried as hard as possible to make me fail. He was unjust and cruel and played dirty. Everyone could see it, and day in and day out, my days were awful. What's worse is I took all of my negative feelings home to my family. No matter how hard I tried to put on a happy face at the end of the day when I walked through the door, something was transferred to my kids. At the time, Rose was almost one year old, and Nick was almost three. When I took him to his bedroom and put him under the covers and he laid his head on the pillow, I asked him how he was feeling. All of a sudden, his lip curled, and he started to cry. It was so sudden that I had no idea what had upset him.

I asked him, "What is the matter?"

He said, "Daddy, I can't be happy."

I immediately asked him why, and he explained, in all of his three-year-old wisdom, that he couldn't be happy because he knew I wasn't happy. I was devastated. His words cut me like a knife. I knew that my actions were causing negative consequences, this time affecting my son.

I discussed the situation with my wife, Maggie, and called my parents for some consultation. This all took place on a Friday, so by Monday morning, I knew what I had to do. At 7:30 a.m. Monday, I walked into my boss's office and told him that I was submitting my resignation. Because I was in a highly visible and consequential position with the company, I allowed some time for him to find a replacement.

Although the resignation never occurred (more on that later), I was resolute that nothing that occurred in the workplace would ever again affect my family in a negative way. I have worked hard at keeping it that way and will continue to do so. A defining moment.

These are just two examples of defining moments in my life. What's important are your defining moments. Can you think of some? Can you see that they helped determine who you are and how you act? Take some time, reflect on your moments, and discuss them with the people who are most important to you. At the very least, it becomes a reaffirmation that important things happen to us and that there is a reason for them happening. And if you're blessed to have trusted friends in your life to discuss moments like this with, you'll learn so much more about them.

CHAPTER 4

HONEST, INTELLIGENT EFFORT IS ALWAYS REWARDED

IT HAS BEEN said that if you do something for two hours each day for five years, you will become an expert at that skill. Now, the most common retort is "But I've done xyz for thirty years, every day, and I'm not an expert!" My question is, and will always remain: Has your effort been both honest and intelligent?

Earlier I mentioned that our family moved from the Bronx, New York City, to a rural town about fifty miles north. Imagine what living in an Italian neighborhood in 1950s Bronx looked like. My parents made the decision that it was safer for the family, especially us boys, if we left the hustle and bustle of city life.

It was a culture shock when we first settled into our new surroundings. We had more trees in the acre behind our house than we had in four square blocks in the city. I had left a place where all of my friends and family lived within two blocks of each other for a place where all I could see was a giant lake. For a time there, I didn't know if I could adjust.

Enter Ricky! He was of Italian heritage, just like my family. He was three years older than me and, because his parents, Mary and Dan, owned a diner, Ricky was on his own during the summer. This was great news for me because I attended the Catholic school in town while Ricky attended the public school. During the year, we only saw each other on Saturdays. But come summer, we spent eight hours a day, six days a week, together.

So what do boys in a small town do during the summer? Baseball, of course! Ricky was a left-handed pitcher, which can be a challenge to catch for. (This was a few years before Pete showed up to play.) I was in need of something to do. Someone suggested that I catch for Ricky. I was hesitant because, even then, he could throw a ninety-plus-miles-per-hour fastball. He had an old catcher's mitt and a mask. For hours on end every day, Ricky would pitch, and I would catch. After a while, he became very good at pitching, and I became very good at catching.

Because Ricky was three years older than I was, he was stronger, faster, and smarter at baseball. Since we spent so much time together, day after day, week after week, I gradually caught up to his level of play—so much so that after only one year of Little League (ages nine through twelve), a coach came to the house and asked my father if he would allow me to play Babe Ruth League (ages thirteen through seventeen). Since I was only ten, my father had reservations. But despite his worries, I begged my father to allow me to play knowing that I was going to be with Ricky the whole time.

My first season in Babe Ruth League was as expected, even though I had been practicing with Ricky. I needed to learn a lot, both physically and mentally, about the fundamentals of baseball. Just being a little husky for my age would not suffice. About half the time a strike-three pitch was thrown, I needed to go retrieve the baseball at the backstop and throw it to first base to complete the out—truly a walk of shame. I had one base hit that entire season. My teammates were very patient with my progression in the sport, mostly due to Ricky. Ricky and I became best friends. Finally, my last time at bat during the last game, I hit a Texas blooper over the second baseman. To my utter joy, the team jumped up and cheered as if it was a game-winning home run.

Was it easy? No. I was giving honest, intelligent effort to something that I loved to do. When possible, I was doing this for more than two hours almost every available day that I could. I was slowly but surely becoming an expert in something. My confidence level, my intellectual level, and my emotional level grew each and every day. I realized that I was becoming good and recognized that I could become better. There came a time when opponents, both coaches and players alike, knew that they weren't going to throw a fastball by me or have a moving pitch that I could not get my bat on. I learned at a very young age that if you really wanted something and were willing to invest the time and effort needed, you could accomplish almost anything. As long as you are taking positive action with a goal in mind, belief in your heart, and passion in your soul, you can achieve it. Again, honest, intelligent effort is always rewarded.

As I said before, Ricky and I became, and continue to be, best friends. But we don't agree on everything. In fact, he tends to lean on the liberal side, while I tend to lean on the conservative side. He is a New York Yankees lover, and I used to be a New York Mets lover. He's American League; I'm National. However, we don't agree to disagree. Rather, we discuss each other's motivation and goals and help each other together. As long as the efforts were honest and intelligent and the end result was worthy and altruistic, we would push and pull each other over the hurdles and through the challenges.

Think how much better our society would be if we set aside our differences and help each other to accomplish a worthy cause. When was the last time we asked someone else what they really wanted to accomplish in life and then helped that person get there? There are different ways of achieving great things. When you help another to do that, they tend to never forget your contribution. More importantly, they are more likely to help others accomplish their worthy goals. This is a lesson that Ricky and I have held on to and continue to promote as we engage with other people. In doing so, we boost our own self-esteem, enhance our confidence, and generally have a positive outlook on life. Honest, intelligent effort is always rewarded!

CHAPTER 5

ENNOBLE NOT EMPOWER

EVERY SO OFTEN in the workplace, I hear from managers, supervisors, and associates that we should empower our people. I don't necessarily disagree; however, I don't think that these employees fully comprehend what they are asking. To empower somebody means to give them the authority or power to do their jobs. Basically, you are suggesting that they have permission to do what is needed to complete what they need to accomplish. Doesn't that go without saying? Can we do better than merely give permission or authority?

Rather than empower people, I suggest that we ennoble others—that is, to elevate or exalt them in their position. If you raise all the people you meet to a level where they rule themselves and are not ruled by you, they take ownership to what they are doing and naturally take responsibility and accountability for their results. Now, this is not about allaying blame for bad work or, for that matter, making things easier. In fact, what I am suggesting is a different dynamic in managing people, and it is more difficult than just empowerment.

So how do we get to ennoblement?

This involves conversation and discussion in finding what is important to the person we are talking to. It's not so much that we communicate what is important to us but rather what motivates the other person. Not all people want more money, power, or status. However, all people are motivated by something—intangible, tangible, or both. In this exchange of ideals, I suggest three common topics: pride, character, and a desire to excel at something.

By pride, I am not talking about boastfulness. I'm talking about those attributes that people hold near and dear to their hearts. It encompasses those qualities that make you feel good about yourself. It's that feeling you get when you walk into a meeting knowing you're dressed for success and have your value proposition down, backward and forward, or when your team comes out of the locker room for a big game, ready to show up and dominate.

By character, I am not considering basic behaviors. I am considering those qualities that cause people to act the way they do. I am an Italian Catholic boy from the Bronx. That has greatly shaped my character. My wife grew up in Ohio with two loving, intellectual, soft-spoken parents. In the same way, that has shaped her character—and some would suggest that her character is a perfect yin to my yang. I guess opposites do attract.

A desire to excel doesn't mean always being number one. Rather, this is a commitment to fully utilizing the talents you have in a positive, altruistic manner. Have you ever taken time out of your day to help a colleague with a task that you're strong at but that they have yet to master, knowing that it will help the organization as a whole? That's a desire to excel. As you can imagine, these discussions involve active, intensive listening and clarification.

Second, after we get to know someone, and it may take considerable time, we then need to challenge people to take control and link their pride, character, and desire to definable activities. Ask these questions: What would you like to do? How would you like to do it? What do you want to accomplish? They may tell you outright, or you may need to ask more open-ended questions. A quick tip: Always pause for a little longer than what's comfortable. People often elaborate much more when you simply remain quiet and actively listen. Once they've conveyed these to you, say, "Have at it!" and "How can I help you?" This shows that you believe in their ability and are willing to help guide them on their journey. Do not be deceived; it is not as simple as it seems. You need to make sure the wants are connected to the qualities and the tasks are within the scope of the job. If so, then you have a foundation to work with. Have at it!

Finally, we do best when we inspect what we expect. Keep in mind these are the activities that were described to you. When we check on how others are progressing, we need to assure each other that we are on the right track. Also remember that you asked, "What can I do to help?" If you were both sincere in your discussions and you grow a deeper understanding of what motivates each other, you will continue to ennoble and motivate.

Here's an example. I had just been promoted into a position that nobody wanted. I was going to be managing a new region. This meant that I would have thirteen managers who reported directly to me. Under those managers were two hundred agents who they oversaw. The environment and the industry were not conducive to profitability, but I was handpicked to turn things around. Everyone likes a good "voluntold" situation, right? To boot, these thirteen seasoned managers and their two hundred equally experienced agents were led to believe that they were the scourge of the company and responsible for the entire region's dreadful results. The sales region ranked thirty-nine out of thirty-nine, and the region ranked thirteen out of thirteen, mostly because of the sales region's performance. So I had to not only get the thirteen managers on board but also make sure they could ennoble their two hundred collective agents as well. As you can imagine, the employees weren't feeling very good about themselves, and the prognosis for the future was dim.

Was that the extent of my challenge? Of course not. The region was in a tough part of Pennsylvania, a state I had never worked in. I was a New Yorker, one of the outsiders. Because the home office specifically asked this outsider to go to a terrible region, a rumor began surfacing that I was only there to shut down sales and clean house. There were bets around the watercoolers that I wouldn't last a year. For me, the only silver lining in this cloud was that I could hardly do worse than what had already been done. The only place to go was up.

My first order of business came as a direct order from the home office. There were three new agents who were six months behind in required performance. As they were part of a new-producer program funded by the company, their performance was closely monitored. Due to their lack of performance, I was told to terminate them immediately. I went to regional management and declined to do so. That went over as well as you can imagine. But I explained that I did not have the opportunity to evaluate how and why they were in that position and that my first act was not going to be one of termination. After much discussion, the regional vice president (VP) reluctantly agreed to give me six months to get them on track, with one caveat—if they failed, I would receive a full charge-back of advanced compensation. This meant that I would be personally charged for money I never received. I accepted the offer.

I left the regional vice president's office and immediately met with the three agents. I asked each of them four questions: "What would you like to do?" "How would you like to do it?" "What do you want to accomplish?" and "What can I do to help?" I got to know what was important to them, what made them tick, what made them proud, what were qualities they had that made them act, and what contributed to their desire to excel. In speaking with them, I knew they had all the equipment—bat, gloves, ball, helmet. They just needed help getting on base. After a good deal of monitoring and measuring by their respective managers, they began to improve. Six months later, they were ahead of plan and succeeding in their roles. I'm happy to report that two of them are still with the organization and one recently retired, all after accomplishing great things.

That's only part of the story. I still had the rest of the sales region to contend with. Turning around the performance of three agents wasn't going to change the rank of the region. My first meeting was with the thirteen sales managers. The tension in the air on that day was palpable. All of them thought they were in trouble of being terminated. Four of them had over twenty years' experience; another five had over ten years' experience; three of them had over five years' experience; and one was in the position for eighteen months. In that meeting, I explained that I could not replace that kind of experience, and I pleaded with all of them not to leave. They were, at best, perplexed.

The news of my actions spread quickly among the agents. It was time to have a meeting. I did not send out an agenda and made no reference to what would be discussed. I simply sent out an invite that included the date, time, and place. Over 95 percent of the producers attended the meeting—that is, 190 people in one room thinking that I was the jerk about to fire them. I was up-front and candid about the situation of the sales region. I explained that we needed to reverse our results and that we needed to do it quickly. I asked if they would share with me (1) what they would like to do, (2) how they would like to do it, (3) what they wanted to accomplish, and (4) what I could do to help. I mentioned that I wanted to get to know them individually and that we, together, would accomplish great things.

After extensive interaction with the producers and the managers, we came up with four principles:

1. Pride in the outfit, confidence in the leadership
2. Unified team effort
3. Positive, winning attitude
4. Fun and fulfillment in what we do

We also came up with how we act:

1. Do what's right.
2. Do the best you can.

3. Follow the Golden Rule: Treat others like you would like to be treated.

And finally we came up with our code: We will not lie, cheat, or steal or tolerate anybody who does.

That is what the sales region was about, doing things right. We would ennoble each other and hold and help each other to a higher standard. We would do things by ourselves, for ourselves.

Six months into the job, I was offered, by the regional and home offices, the opportunity to have every one of our clients receive an underwriting questionnaire. Our pleasure-use and new-home discounts were in the 89 percent and 81 percent range, respectively. This meant that 89 percent of our policyholders drove less than eight thousand miles per year, and 81 percent of our homes were less than fourteen years old. Research suggested that 39 percent and 29 percent ranges were more appropriate. Working through the managers, we decided to put the responsibility on ourselves and the producers. We called a meeting, gave them the facts, and allowed them sixty days to change the results. Two months later, the region was at 31 percent and 23 percent, respectively. We were well within the guidelines.

More importantly than achieving the correct ratios, the agents, working with the supervision of their managers, took control of their own affairs. We explained the situation and asked them, "What would you like to do?" "How would you like to do it?" "What do you want to accomplish?" and "What could we do to help?" The profitability results changed in the right direction, and the sales region was viewed as part of the solution for the enterprise—not the cause of the problem. Every person felt a sense of accomplishment. Within three years, we were ranked the third-best sales region in the organization and continued moving forward in a positive direction. In my fourth year, I was asked to take a promotion to lead the sales function of the entire region and later, when we combined two regions, the entire state. Applying the same principles, the region went from thirteen to one and remained there for another four years. I'd like to take the credit, but that wasn't the case. It was all of us, ennobling each other as a team, that got us where we were.

CHAPTER 6

WHEN ALL ELSE FAILS, USE COMMON SENSE, EVEN THOUGH IT IS NOT PART OF THE PROGRAM

RULES, RULES, RULES. We are all given rules to follow. If you don't follow the rules, you're in trouble. If you don't know the rules, you're in trouble. If you know the rules and purposely choose not to follow them, you're in *big* trouble. For the most part, rules are codes of conduct and are necessary for order and good behavior in society. In our workplace, rules are procedural and tell us what we can and can't do. However, in some situations, the rules should be challenged.

Allow me to elaborate. Remember that promotion I got for the regional position? In this region, there were three sales districts that reported to the regional sales superintendent. On a Friday in late November of 1989, I was called up by the regional vice president, Phil, and was asked to meet him at his home at 9:00 a.m. on Monday. Naturally, I assumed the worst. After all, he was my boss's boss, and he wanted to meet me at his house—two hours away and not in the regional office. He was adamant that I was not to be seen by any other employees, and I was held to the strictest confidentiality concerning the phone call and further discussions. Over the entire weekend, I agonized thinking of all the possible scenarios. I had my wife and son at home and another one on the way. Of all the times to get read the riot act and fired, this was the worst time.

I arrived at 8:45 a.m. at Phil's residence. Forcing a smile on my face, I said hello to his wife, Ruth, and was graciously asked if I would like anything, a cup of coffee or a glass of water. I politely declined and was given a seat in the living room. Phil came down from upstairs and took a seat across from me. He was suitably social and, not being one to mince words, quickly got to the point. He asked me if I had given any thought to why he asked for a meeting. I said that I did give serious thought for the call but came to no conclusion.

He asked me to explain how we achieved our sales regional results during the last two years, and I described, in detail, all the actions we took to move forward. He recalled that I was asked to terminate three new producers and I had challenged the home office, telling them that it was not appropriate to do so at that time. He reminded me that I had put myself in jeopardy, both financially and professionally. I reminded him that, even though the rules were put into place to have the program managed consistently, it was the right thing to do to investigate why all three were not performing if the new-producer program had been administered correctly. An in-depth review suggested that the company was lax in its implementation. Phil agreed, and he then congratulated me on turning around the results, receiving the bonuses, and moving along without any fanfare or self-adulation. Phil then wanted me to explain my feelings toward challenging hard-line rules. I explained that the situation called for me to evaluate what occurred, to examine the details of why it occurred, and to make a decision as to how to proceed. After that, it became evident that common sense dictated to move slowly.

He agreed and then informed me that my boss had decided to retire at the end of the year, and he asked if I would be interested in interviewing for the vacant regional position. This thought never entered my mind, and I was unprepared to give an answer. So I reacted and said that it was beyond my imagination that I would be considered. Secretly I questioned if he had the authority to offer me this opportunity. After all, I understood the "rules" to be that I would have to go back to the home office as a director for a period of time and then be offered a similar position in a different region. Phil asked me if I was trying to blow the opportunity. He chose this time to inform me that the CEO had already given permission for the interview. This CEO was the same person who told me three and a half years earlier that I had ten years to straighten out the profitability of the sales region. Ultimately, I was offered the position, and I accepted it. Phil wanted somebody who knew the rules but, if needed, would insist on considering alternatives for the better good of all. Three months later another scenario evolved.

I was managing the entire region, and I had not yet hired my replacement in the sales region I had vacated. I was given numerous candidates from the home office to interview, but none of these people possessed the intricate qualities to manage thirteen sales managers and two hundred agents.

Remember, no one wanted the position when it ranked last in the company and had profitability problems. Now, everybody was interested. Enter Bob.

I first met Bob in 1984 as sales-management-development manager in the home office. He was assigned to the business region and became one of the instructors in the sales-management schools, teaching how to lead others in selling in the commercial arena. He was bigger than life and was always willing to lend a helping hand. He never met a person he didn't like. We became more than associates and quickly became friends. As a matter of fact, he met his future bride at a party I hosted. By now, I had been removed from my home office stint for almost four years. While being introduced to the sales regions, I had found that Bob had taken an agency opportunity in our most central sales region. He was located only a few miles from the regional office. This confused me because if there was ever a person who was best suited for managing others, it was Bob. Why did he become an individual producer?

At the sales region kickoff, I was introduced as the new regional sales superintendent. This came to everyone as big a surprise as it was to me. At these meetings, I always had an open question-and-answer session. During this session, Bob asked some pointed and poignant questions about how I could handle them, but I was taken aback that they came from Bob. This was not in his DNA, and it bothered me that he changed in such a drastic fashion. I thought about it at great length, and a week later, I decided to meet with him one-on-one in his office. I walked in unannounced and shared my observations. He immediately apologized for the tone of his questions and agreed that I was correct in mentioning that this seemed out of character for him.

Bob was bitter. He deeply wanted to be promoted from the home office but was constantly overlooked because corporate came up with a hard-and-fast rule that college education was a requirement at certain levels in the organization. Bob's experience alone could not be manufactured in twenty years of college education. I wanted to do something, but what? He was never going to be happy as a producer—successful, but not happy. On my way back to the office, I thought what a great fit he would be for my replacement in our easternmost sales region. I decided to discuss the possibility with Phil.

Here we go again. I wasn't in the job for three months, and I was asking for an exception on another hard-and-fast rule from the home office. We knew this was not going to be received with open arms, but after substantial discussion, Phil allowed me to interview to determine interest, without any promises to hire. Also, I needed to tell Bob that this was a long shot. I set up an appointment and interviewed Bob two days later. His first reaction was the same as mine was when Phil had interviewed me; he figured that I would never get permission. I told him that I'd like to try.

I've already discussed that as I get to know people, I like to discuss pride, character, and their desire to excel. As expected, Bob rated highly in these areas. However, when I'm in the posture of hiring, I also want to discuss challenges that people have experienced. This tells me a few things—most importantly, if the candidates can handle what's about to come at them in this role. There are jobs in this industry that will bring people to their knees, and this was one of those jobs.

Quite simply, I ask a person, "What was the hardest thing you ever had to deal with?" Answers range from the benign, such as getting a C grade in college, to heavier subject material, such as handling a divorce or being let go from a job. No matter what the answer, my next questions are "How did you handle the adversity?" "What actions did you take?" "What was the final outcome?" and "What did you learn?" These are the most important questions because everyone faces hardships and trials. What's important is how you get through it and how you learn from the experience. So I asked Bob those questions. Remember, I explained that we were friends in the home office, and I thought we knew a good amount about each other. But what he was about to tell me was something I never knew and never could have guessed. He confided that he was born with a deadly gene—one that would transfer to his sons and lower their life expectancy to age eighteen. He went on to say that he and his wife had sons, and they died before age twenty. After considerable agonizing—and being faith-based—he and his spouse decided to try one more time. They gave birth to a daughter, whom they named Angel because she was truly a gift from heaven. I was assured that there was nothing that could happen in the new role that Bob could not handle.

Getting the exception was long and hard, but I knew it was worth the effort. Three months after my initial interview, Phil and I were in a meeting where our CEO was attending. I was directly asked when I was going to hire my replacement. I quickly and directly answered, "When I get the exception to hire Bob." Our CEO called over the president of the company (also a friend of Bob), and our president said he knew Bob well and didn't have a problem with moving forward. We set up an appointment for Phil to interview him—after all, it was a presidential exception. In the interview, Bob told Phil that he could learn a lot from me and that I could learn a lot from him. Phil was blown away and made the offer on the spot. *When all else fails, use common sense, even though it's not part of the program.*

CHAPTER 7

MAKE EVERY EVENT A GREAT EVENT

WHATEVER WE DO, whenever we do it, we have a choice. Whether we are alone or with others, we control the way we respond. That sounds pretty logical and easily understandable. However, let's think about this: Consider that what we do and what we don't do, what we say and what we don't say, and how we act or how we don't act have an effect on the final result or outcome. I'm sure you heard before that practice makes perfect. However, if you practice something badly, then the intended result is a far cry from what you actually achieve. Practice doesn't make perfect; perfect practice makes perfect. Remember, honest, intelligent effort is always rewarded!

So let's apply this to our everyday activities. How can we ensure we are doing things right? It is a choice. We can choose to act and react, or we can think in the moment, pause for a second, and use our time and talent to achieve the most desired result. This is not easily accomplished, yet with a little "perfect practice," it is achievable. Take, for example, an instance where we receive a phone call. How do we handle that call? When we answer, what is our greeting? Do we just say "hello," or do we have some other greeting? Do we mention our names and ask how can we help? Do we answer the phone the same way every time? Most importantly, do we understand that the way we answer the phone has consequences, either good or bad?

I understand we are in a time when caller ID allows us to know the caller. We can choose to take the call or not answer. No matter the situation, if we choose to answer, we set the tone by our salutation. It goes without saying that we treat family and friends differently than the rest of society, but do we truly understand the importance of our greeting? In addition, how do we manage the remainder of the call? I think you would be surprised about how your phone conversation is received by the caller.

While training producers and new sales managers, I often had the opportunity to tape training calls. Even when the trainees knew that the simulation was being taped, they were surprised and, in most cases, taken aback as to how they wanted to be received compared to what actually occurred. When given candid feedback by the participants, the trainees were astounded that what they intended in the conversation was not realized by the receiver.

Now, we really don't want to take this too far. We have our own personalities, along with accents, tempo, emphasis, and style. The worst thing that can happen is we answer the phone and sound like a recording. I am not suggesting that we retool our approach to answering the phone. I do recommend that we are conscious and cognizant of the opportunity to separate ourselves from the rest of society and that the choice is ours. What we do or say, as well as how we act, matters greatly in the end.

It boils down to this: Make every event a great event. We're not just talking about a phone call—a simple interaction between two or more people. We are talking about being conscious and cognizant of the situation and taking the time to devote your energy to the moment, not the papers on the desk or the kids in the background. It may be better to explain to the caller that another time would be more appropriate to converse. Also, if you are the caller, you should have insight and understanding that it is not a convenient time for your phone call. I appreciate, when being called, that I am asked, "Is this a good time to chat?"

We can choose to make the best of any situation, good or bad. Let's go back to 1968. I was a junior attending an all-boys Catholic high school. It was my last class in late spring, and my English teacher, a wise priest, was finishing the lesson. A fellow classmate and I were having a side conversation, and we were called out by our teacher. Now, the usual punishment was detention after school, sitting in a room with other errant classmates, and that would last about forty-five minutes to an hour. However, this wise priest knew that we both were on an athletic team, and our punishment would be no more than possibly running a mile after practice. Therefore, we were given an assignment due in class the next day. My classmate was to write an essay on "the sex life of a piece of chalk," while mine was "What's inside a Ping-Pong ball?" The essays would be read, to our embarrassment, in front of the class the next day. *Not* funny.

I was not a happy camper. I took the train every day to school in White Plains, New York. It was a two-hour journey, door to door, and I had regular homework to do, not to mention going to baseball practice. I also had to tell my parents what happened in class. Practice was taken care of after school, and homework was completed on the train—but there was no way I could complete this essay in secret.

Now for the assignment. While eating dinner, I explained my predicament, and my father suggested making the best of a bad situation. In essence, he figured that the essay was justified and fair and that we may have an opportunity to have some fun in completing the task. We concluded that, it being for an English class, we could compose a poem. With all apologies to Edgar Allan Poe and Lord Byron, here is the finished product:

I was given a dollar for doing a chore,
So I took myself to a neighborhood store.
As I wandered through the aisles and mall,
My fantasy was taken by a Ping-Pong ball.
The urge to purchase I could not fake,
So I surrendered, and it was mine to take.
Back at home in my room at the wing,
I pondered on this strange happening.
As I nodded nearly napping,
Suddenly there came a rapping,
As of someone gently tapping,
Tapping inside my Ping-Pong ball.
"Who art thou inside my Ping-Pong ball?" I uttered.
"Is this some nefarious scheme?" I muttered.
And unsheathing my trusty snickersnee,

I sliced my Ping-Pong ball in three.
When, lo and behold, from the midst of the parts
Arose a most beautiful damsel of superior arts.
Long blond tresses and about five foot three
With peaches and cream complexion was she.
"I am the genie within the sphere,
Who was locked inside for many a year.
I'm yours to command, oh Master Mine!
What is your wish, your end design?"
Thus, I found, once and for all,
What's inside a Ping-Pong ball.

Assignment completed! It was past bedtime, and I was tired from the day. However, lying down and contemplating the occurrences of the last seven hours, I realized that from that punishment, I went from dejection to elation, and it was all because of how I reacted to the situation. I chose to make this a great event.

The next day in class, we were called upon to read our essays. As expected, my classmate had a difficult time with his assignment and was embarrassed. I, on the other hand, was excited that it was my turn to stand in front of my classmates. I read the poem with enthusiasm, and when I was finished, there were about ten seconds of silence followed by clapping and shouting. More to the point, the wise priest had a grin from ear to ear with one comment: "Well done." My reading of the poem spread throughout the school like a wildfire, and before practice ended that day, I was approached by teachers and students alike. Think about it: We all have a choice for how we want to handle each and every event in our lives. For those who take the time and apply their talents, great things can happen. For those who operate in cruise control, the results are less attractive. Make every event a great event. The choice is yours.

CHAPTER 8

TIME IS VALUABLE

I STARTED WITH this company in May 1974. However, in actuality, I was introduced to this company in 1959. My father had a job in New York City and commuted to work over fifty miles one way, every day. Although he shared the ride with three other commuters, the strain was affecting him both physically and emotionally. After a bout with diverticulitis and a two-day hospital stay, my father decided to pursue other avenues of employment.

In his search, he met a young manager, Charlie, who suggested he consider insurance sales. Charlie had interviewed my dad and was impressed with his ability to converse with other people. After a final interview with Charlie's superior, George, the three agreed that the opportunity should be pursued. My father's original intent was to try insurance sales on a part-time basis. Thirty-seven years later, Dad retired from the company, with an agency that was recognized as a premier asset in his hometown—so much so that his manager at that time chose to succeed him and take over the reins.

As I mentioned, this started a new chapter in our lives and was an integral part of our family in 1959. My dad's first office was a converted porch attached to the rear of our house. We only had one phone, and when policyholders called, we were expected to answer the phone promptly and courteously and take any message they wanted passed on. Keep in mind, there were no computers in 1959, and sales were made after normal business hours and usually involved face-to-face meetings with both spouses. Many of these occurred on our converted back porch, and it was made clear to all of us that visitors would be treated with the utmost respect. The customer always came first.

In addition to those tenets, the company was extremely family oriented. Charlie would visit my dad often and always took time to talk with my mom and us kids. He always asked how we were doing and often showed his appreciation of our family support for our father's new endeavor. On occasion, he would bring little treats, maybe brownies or cookies. I even remember, on a hot summer day, the Good Humor man drove up in his ice cream truck, and we were each allowed to purchase an item. Charlie paid.

It was clear that my father's manager was there to help him grow a business showing us, in deed rather than word, that we were all part of Dad's future success. One day, our submersible water pump broke and, as you can imagine, needed to be fixed quickly. My dad went to the store, purchased the pump and necessary attachments, and started digging to get access. As my father, my brother Richard, and I were digging and moving dirt, Charlie pulled into the driveway. After ascertaining the situation, Charlie asked for some of my dad's work clothes, changed from his suit, and proceeded to help. We all were very appreciative.

When the job was finished, Charlie, my dad and mom, and the three children sat around and had cool glasses of lemonade. Charlie actually took a shower and dressed back into his suit. Before leaving, he made it a point to have a discussion with my mom and dad. I was fortunate enough to hear the conversation. Charlie asked my dad how much it would have been to have a plumber come over and install a new pump. My dad said $400. Charlie then asked how much he saved by doing it himself. My dad said $120. Charlie then asked if something went wrong with the pump, who would be responsible to fix the problem. My dad said that he would. Then Charlie reiterated that if the plumber had installed the new pump and something went wrong, the plumber would be responsible to fix the problem. Charlie asked my dad how many hours it took to get the pump and install it with his help. My dad admitted that it was about eight hours. Charlie went on to explain that if my dad spent that time preparing and presenting supplemental student-accident policies (policies that my father had great success with in the community), all he would have to do is sell nine cases.

It was a lesson that I would never forget. Sure, insurance sales are not for the fainthearted. They are difficult, and sometimes you need to give yourself a break from the action. So if you are doing a chore, such as fixing some plumbing, that is somewhat therapeutic, then have at it. However, if the chore is truly a chore, then you may want to consider spending time doing what you do best, and let others do what they do best. I always admired Charlie and appreciated how he extended himself to his producers. These were lessons that I always wanted to convey to my producers, managers who I supervised, and peers who I worked with. We all learned at a young age that the customer was number one and that lending a helping hand went a long way toward the results that you achieved.

CHAPTER 9

DON'T FEED THE ANIMALS

OFTEN, WHEN WE are out and about, we'll come upon a sign that says, "Don't Feed the Animals." It could be at a zoo, someone's property, or an animal shelter. I'd like to suggest that there is one particular animal that you never want to feed. It is the turkey buzzard. You've probably seen them on the side of the road eating roadkill. You'll see them in groups. They feast on the carcass, regurgitate it, and then eat that. To most people, they are repulsive. However, many people don't realize how much we are surrounded by these birds.

There are people in our lives who survive on the frailties, misfortunes, faults, and weaknesses of others. They meet in groups and abase anyone and everyone, with one goal in mind—to destroy another's composure, well-being, and esteem. These people take particular delight in hurting others and possibly ruining one's reputation. If you're not part of their group, they despise you.

Throughout my career, I have had the pleasure of being introduced to and working with numerous people. I've always tried to look at the good in others. I think that every person has a goodness within them to make the world a better place. Whether in spiritual, social, or work environments, people are generally good. It wasn't until my late twenties and early thirties that I realized how naive I was.

As I was interviewing for a promotional opportunity in the home office, I was introduced to an individual who quickly led me to believe that he supported me getting the opportunity for which I was interviewing. He suggested that I would be an asset to the team and that we would work well together. Within weeks, we were working together in building a solid division in sales-management development. It wasn't long after that I found this person had an insidious nature. He would find the faults in others, especially our supervisor, and always share how he could do better. He would never make any comments to these people face-to-face, but rather always behind their backs. He was adamant that if you didn't agree with him, you would not be part of the team. He preyed on those of weaker personalities. A real turkey buzzard.

Within two years, we were both promoted to the same position in different sections of the country, reporting to a new boss. Nothing changed, and he did everything he could to malign our mutual supervisor and garner our combined support against him. I chose not to play.

Now, our supervisor reported to a regional VP. In an effort to debase our supervisor and knowing that he did not have all of our support, this person decided to make a case with a home office VP over and above the regional VP. The case was flimsy and contrived, and three of us were called into the regional VP's office. When questioned concerning what happened, two of us had nothing to say, and the person responsible for the problem spoke in generalities. We were admonished and told that nothing like this should ever happen again. Later, in the men's room, I confronted this person and told him that I had enough of his antics. We each understood that we were not on the same page.

A little over a year later, our supervisor retired, and I was promoted to the position in the same region. This, of course, meant that I was now supervising the person who caused the dissension among the group. Like nothing ever happened, he now pursued the same course of action against me. He solicited the team to work hard at having them work against me. Again, with a flimsy, contrived position, he went against the person I hired to replace me and challenged my decision-making with human resources. We were still working for the regional vice president when the topic came up for discussion in a cabinet meeting. The regional VP blew his top and ordered the human resources manager and me to terminate this employee.

In an earlier chapter, I mentioned my relationship with this VP and explained to him that I was reluctant to terminate on these grounds. You see, I realized he was a turkey buzzard who survived by making other people look bad so that he could look good. Phil, the VP, wanted nothing of it and told me to proceed with termination. In a final, desperate attempt, I solicited help from Phil's wife, Ruth. She interceded on my behalf, and Phil acquiesced. He did remind me that I would regret it and someday would be stabbed in the back by this person. The next day, we went up to visit the employee and relayed the entire story. Years later, I realized

Phil was right, and I was stabbed in the back. The good news is it had no effect on me, but it had an adverse effect on the person.

The moral of the story is (1) to look good by being good and not by making others look bad and (2) to avoid turkey buzzards like the plague. All they will do is bring you down, sap your energy, diminish your self-esteem, and alienate you from others who recognize what you are doing. But don't be surprised when people act like people. I still feel good that I did not terminate that employee. Ultimately, he terminated himself. Nevertheless, treat everybody with empathy, sensitivity, and concern. That's the winning formula.

CHAPTER 10

DO WHAT YOU DO BEST, RATHER THAN WHAT SOMEBODY ELSE DOES POORLY

IN CHAPTER 1, we discussed embracing your uniqueness. I would like to expand upon that with relationship to one's talents. The talents we acquire are a gift from God. Sure, it takes time to recognize our talents and even more time to cultivate them. However, they are a gift, and our gift back to God is using those talents for positive results. They are unique to the individual, and no two people have exactly the same talents.

Throughout my career, I have been asked to allow people to shadow me in my daily business activities. Basically, I would pick up these people in the morning, and they would follow me throughout the business day. They would see my interaction with agents, associates, peers, and customers. In between business, we used our time in the car to discuss our activities. The intent was for them to see firsthand how the job was being done. This is a good thing—only if the people who shadowed me recognized that it was up to them to fit these activities into their personality and talents. It would be of little use to them to mimic me.

Among the activities to be observed was conducting a district meeting. This is where the agents assemble as a group, and the manager trains, develops, and motivates the participants on a myriad of topics. For every hour of a meeting, I spent approximately three hours in preparation. Rather than tell-and-do management, I tried intently to lead the group to self-discovery. This required knowing your topic well and preparing for a plethora of questions to be asked by the attendees. I prepared for meetings the way a lawyer prepares for court—know your stuff, know the possible questions, no surprises. This is harder than it seems. In addition to knowing the questions, you have to anticipate all possible answers, including those that could take you off track and what questions were needed to get them back in the right direction. If done correctly, the end result was the participants' ownership in applying their newfound message. In addition to this, I developed a motivational ending to each meeting, and all participants, including guests, left feeling good about themselves, both individually and collectively as a team.

After one such meeting, the person who was shadowing me was visibly upset that she could not do, in any form, what I had just done in my meeting. I quickly explained to her that she should not even consider trying. After all, her experiences were completely different than mine, and our personalities were not the same. After an hour discussion, we decided that she should conduct her meetings utilizing her unique talents and not attempting to copy mine. Although we both desired the same end result, she could do it better if she incorporated her personality and applied her talents. I am happy to say that this woman grew to become one of the best managers in the company and one of the best presenters at corporate meetings.

One final thought in recognizing your personality, talents, and one true self: You are not in it alone. I love golf! The reason I love this sport is you need to find your own one true swing, and nobody else has your swing. We all have different sizes, shapes, strengths, experiences, and areas that need improvement. You never have the same golf shot, lie of the golf ball, or external conditions. Yet the key to being successful is consistency, and the key to consistency is allowing trusted advisers to make suggestions. In order to be a trusted adviser, that person has to have some familiarity with your one true swing.

So how do you do this? You spend hours and hours practicing, to find what works best for you. Then, you solicit others' advice about how you can improve. In many cases, you go to a teaching professional, and he or she suggests removing bad "death moves." Mostly, you play a lot with people who know you because you let them get to know you. When things go bad, as they often do with golf, your advisers help you out.

This works the same way in other aspects of life. Let people get to know you, the one true you. When you get out of kilter, allow them to make suggestions to get you back in sync. Understand your talents, and work hard at mastering them to provide positive results. Do what you do best. And remember, honest, intelligent effort is always rewarded.

CHAPTER 11

TO THINE OWN SELF BE TRUE

NOW THIS IS a tough one. I am sure that most people have heard "to thine own self be true" at least once in their lifetime. At first glance, this seems pretty straightforward—in fact, Shakespeare originally wrote it as a joke. What other choice do you have other than to be true to yourself? Yet unless you have the parts and pieces of your life in order, it feels almost impossible to achieve. It can be difficult to be true to yourself. Part of the reason it is difficult to be true to yourself is the fact that you must first "know thyself." All of us may think we know what we want. But how many times have you gotten what you thought you wanted, yet you still weren't as happy as you thought you'd be? Instead, reflect on some questions: What makes you tick? What charges your batteries? What do you stand for? Against? Are your priorities in sync? By reflecting on these, we become enlightened to be true to ourselves.

The more I get to know myself, the more I understand that who I am is related to who I am yet to become. I am sixty-nine years old and still learning that I am the artist and that I am the clay. I ask, "What am I making of myself?" I choose! My choices reveal my values. My choices are either good or bad. My choices have consequences. I am the product of my choices.

We are unique! We are individuals. We have a name. We continue to write our stories as we live our lives. We are human beings, and in being so, we are imperfect. Perfection is impossible on an individual basis. However, we get closer to perfection when we work together, possibly as a couple, a family, a team, a community, or a generation. Only when we truly understand our own imperfections do we begin to recognize the best in others. It will always be a case of us realizing that we would strive for perfection, knowing full well perfection comes in God's time and not ours.

It is natural to experience ups and downs, peaks and valleys, and trials and tribulations in life. It is a never-ending growing process of moving ourselves from our comfort zones into new, unchartered waters. It is a nearly impossible task when done alone, and it can only be accomplished with the help of others—parents, trusted friends and advisers, spouses, coaches, teachers. Also, it becomes imperative that we become good examples for our children, families, friends, and associates.

Sure, we will make mistakes, and that is human too. However, if we learn from our mistakes, then we become stronger and better, as long as there is a resolve not to make the same mistakes again. I have often told business associates that if they weren't making mistakes, then they weren't working hard enough. As long as people were up-front and honest about making the mistake and learned not to make it again,

I had no problem with it. When you do have a problem is when people spend their time, talent, and resources looking for and embellishing on the faults of others. This is the antithesis of growth—and it makes you a turkey buzzard.

There is no courage in making people feel small and insignificant. In my opinion, it is one of the most serious sins we can commit. Dwelling on the darkness in society serves no one. Let your light shine for everyone. Don't look for the problems, but rather create solutions. We are all meant to shine, to excel in what we love to do. Don't ever let another person bring you down to a level where you are uncomfortable. Find something that you love doing, something that completes you, and go after it with a passion that excites others. You will become a magnet for people who yearn for a piece of what you have.

My wish for others is that whatever they do in life is captivating and not insulating. As the Serenity Prayer goes, "God, grant me the serenity to accept the things I cannot change, courage to change the things I can, and wisdom to know the difference." Grasp and concentrate on the moment, and seize the opportunity at hand. Don't dwell on the past with all its failures, and don't live in the future with all its empty promises; rather, stay grounded recognizing your place in a continuously changing world. Work every day on enhancing current relationships and building new ones.

I have been both lucky and blessed in my life when people, for no explicable reason, took an interest in me. In fifth, sixth, and seventh grades, I and a classmate, a good friend, were chosen by our parish pastor, Monsignor Sweeney, to serve his daily Mass. That's right, Mass 365 days a year. We were chosen because our Latin was impeccable (Masses were in Latin those days), and we knew how to set up the altar for Mass. After Mass, we walked to the diner in town to have breakfast, and after eating, we went either to school (when in session) or home (during the summer months). It so happened that a company named Guidepost had its headquarters in Carmel, New York, and often the CEO of that company went to the diner for coffee before he started his day. He was always accompanied by his cronies from Guidepost. After a while, he asked me why I was in the diner every day around the same time. I explained the reason why. This gentleman took an interest in me, and he enjoyed conversing with me about life's lessons.

That person was Norman Vincent Peale, and I didn't realize who he was until I was in college. Of the topics we discussed, the one that imbedded in my head was one that I heard many times later in my life from different people. We are what we think—we act how we think, and our achievements and relationships reflect our thoughts. Think about it. Basically, by learning how to think correctly and taking the time to reflect on what we choose to be integrally important, we fashion what we will become. We act accordingly and somewhat control the results we experience. The beauty is if we don't like the results we get, we might want to change the way we think. Are our priorities in order? Are we on a path that feels right? If not, what do we do about it?

Think of our life source as if it is a free-flowing river. Are we channeling the river in the right direction? Are we keeping it free from pollutants? Are we allowing new, fresh, pure, and plentiful waters to enter? Are we using these waters for the greater good and sharing our life source with others who may need it? Are we treating the river as a resource, not wasting its limited supply on foolish labors? The choice is ours, and we, ultimately, determine the path we take.

CHAPTER 12

KEYS TO BUILDING RELATIONSHIPS

THE INSURANCE INDUSTRY is different than any other industry in the country. I think that we forget that there are many countries in the world that do not have insurance, at least in the manner and form that we have in the United States. One of the reasons that our country is so strong economically and financially is because of the insurance industry's ability to preserve, protect, and create wealth. I learned early on that selling insurance is a noble profession. To be successful, you must care about people. If you don't, you will not be successful, and worse yet, you will give the industry a bad name. The bottom line is to be successful in selling insurance, you must develop long-term relationships of trust and confidence.

Let's take a deeper look at that statement. *Long-term* means you're not peddling policies, and decisions are made with long-lasting stability and consistency in mind. If coverages and contracts change every few years, you're in trouble. *Trust* means that there will be no surprises and that, first and foremost, the needs of the client are addressed. The benefits to the client are paramount to the benefits to the producer and company. If you fail at gaining the trust of the client, if for one moment the prospect questions your candor or sincerity, you're in trouble. Lastly, you must give evidence that you know what you are talking about with the features of the product and that these coverages align best with the suitability and needs of the client. If you cannot convey that a particular item is needed or unneeded, you're in trouble.

So what do you need to be successful in developing a long-term relationship of trust and confidence with a client? First, you need time—time to get to know the client, time to give the appropriate effort and energy to the sale, and time to keep at it. You must collect all the information you need in the decision-making process. After obtaining that data, you must study it and develop your recommendations around the needs of the client. Then, you must understand that there are two sales being made: one to the prospect and the other to the company. If you don't take the time to do all of these activities, you will fall short of your desired result.

Next, you need skill. You need to be the best at knowing how, what, who, when, where, and, most importantly, why. You need to invest in yourself—in learning, presenting, following through, and servicing.

Finally, you need courage. It takes a special type of person to sell insurance products, and not everyone is suited for the career. In fact, a study done by LIMRA in 1984 shows that for every seventeen people who try to enter into the industry, only one succeeds past five years. Understand that 85 percent of the working population has to be told what to do and when to do it, 15 percent can run their own affairs, and only 2 percent of that 15 percent can lead others. The industry is in desperate need of more of that 2 percent.

So let's talk about how to develop a relationship with anyone and not just with a prospective client. Strong relationships are rare, and we should not confuse acquaintances with strong relationships. In my experience, there are many differentiating aspects. I suggest that before anybody decides to spend their time, talent, and resources on developing a new relationship, they check their references. This sounds self-serving, and it is. If I'm going to share what makes me tick, what charges my batteries, and what I stand for or against, then I am going to want to know as much as is appropriate about who I share my feelings with. In finding out what makes them tick, what charges their batteries, and what they stand for and against, you must ask a lot of the questions. In fact, I strongly suggest that you never ever make a statement when you can get to the same place by asking a question. This goes a long way in understanding what motivates people, and then the development of a relationship starts. More importantly, you learn much more by asking than by telling.

Do not discount the value and reward of a strong relationship with a good friend. These are not easy to come by, and it takes much work and effort to begin and sustain one. However, if you do, then you have something special. I mentioned the challenge I had when I was a regional sales manager in the area that was last in the company. It was a mess, and the sales region was losing a significant amount of money. The task put me to my knees. We had to make tough decisions, and the manager, originally from New York, coming from the home office, was not immediately embraced by thirteen sales managers and two hundred agents. Enter Dave, a sales administration manager who took the time to get to know me and, without me asking, took it upon himself to talk with the influential sales managers and agents in the sales region. His opinion was highly regarded, and he suggested to the sales managers and agents that they give me a chance because he personally felt that I was going to act in their best interest.

We called for a meeting, and it was fully attended. I explained the situation and told them that I needed time to wrap my hands around the problem. I asked them to be patient and promised them that two things would occur: (1) the minute we knew what direction to take, we would communicate with them; and (2) we would assist them in following a successful path, assuring them that the problem was not their fault. My intent was to elevate their status to a high level of respect and esteem within the company. As you know, the rest is history. Within three years, the managers and agents in those five counties were revered. All of this occurred because Dave took the time to get to know me and, in doing so, urged the players to give the regional manager a chance. The managers and agents would have never attended this meeting had Dave not advocated for me.

If Dave and I never developed a strong relationship of trust and confidence, we could have never sold our plan to the sales region. Our success ennobled both of us to build many more strong relationships with good people.

Fourteen years later, I made a difficult decision to leave the company and start my own consulting business after moving to Virginia. Dave was now a regional sales manager in Virginia, and he was in dire need of having a strong manager take over one of the most influential districts in the company. When he found out that I was now in Northern Virginia, he sought me out and spent the better part of three months trying to convince me to come back to the company and run the district. He and his wife would talk with me and my wife, and they were so persistent that I acquiesced and took the opportunity. The real reason for taking the job was not Dave's persistence, but rather, deep down, I knew he had my best interests at heart. Was it a good decision? Absolutely!

When Dave presented the paperwork, it was met with significant resistance. In fact, some suggested that I was not eligible for rehire. Dave fought it so vigorously that a meeting was called for Dave and me to visit with the regional vice president, Mark. After extensive discussion, Mark concluded that he, personally, was in agreement with Dave and that the rehire would be approved. That was the start of another strong relationship. We quickly learned each other's talents, we recognized each other's strengths and areas of improvement, and most importantly we pulled each other through tough situations. Mark was able to rekindle a fire inside me that had been lost many years before. He allowed me the freedom to use my imagination, ingenuity, and initiative to accomplish great things, and we flourished. Mark ultimately became, and remains, the president of the property and casualty company, and at that, we were always available if one of us needed the other. Yes, strong relationships of trust and confidence are rare. But when you have one, hold onto it tightly; for the experience is one you'll never forget.

CHAPTER 13

JUST SHOW UP

A FEW YEARS ago, I had the opportunity to meet up with Joe, a man I had known for some fifty years. He had just turned ninety, and he was interested in learning how I was doing, how my life progressed, and if I was the same person he met when I was in my twenties. After about thirty minutes of sharing my life's story, he found out that I was no longer a spitfire twenty-year-old kid and that I, like most people, had matured from college ideologies to real-life actualities. He smiled and shared that he was happy that my life turned out exactly how he thought it would fifty years ago. I, too, was interested in learning his perspective about how his life progressed.

I knew a little of Joe's background. As a child in New York, he was brought up in a Catholic orphanage. As one could imagine, his childhood was not a bed of roses, but Joe recognized that he was fortunate to have people who cared about him. He persevered, and when he was of age, he decided to join the army. He was accepted into the intelligence corps and became a specialist in decrypting coded messages.

He knew he was smart, and he utilized that talent wisely. While at the Catholic home, he was introduced to his future wife, Josephine. She was a kind soul who saw the good in all people. Their love for each other was clearly evident to those who were lucky enough to meet them. They started their lives in the South Bronx, moved to upstate New York, and had eight children (four boys and four girls), each having different personalities—for real, eight different personalities. The only common denominator among the children was the deep love they had for each other, taught by two loving parents. When you walked in the house, you were welcomed with smiles and warm greetings.

Back to Joe! For forty years, he worked in a clothing business. Each day, he would wake up very early in the morning and drive over one hundred miles to various businesses, delivering all sorts of uniforms, taking new orders, and when time permitted, finding new customers. After twelve-hour days, he would return home to his family eagerly waiting for dinner. Think of it, eight chirping birds waiting at the table for Dad to arrive and for Mom to serve dinner, which was a special time for the family—a time to eat, a time to share, a time to clap, a time to laugh, and, yes, a time to cry. I never once heard Joe raise his voice in anger, and the only time there was scolding was on the rare occasion when one of the eight would potentially disrespect Mother. When Josephine passed, a piece of Joe went with her. He shared that sometimes he gets to talk with her, but nevertheless, he dearly misses her.

As Joe and I talked, I asked him if he had any regrets, fully expecting to hear that he didn't. To my surprise, he lamented that he wished he learned earlier in life that he could have accomplished much more if he only knew that the people above him were no wiser, no more intelligent, or no stronger than he was. I respectfully disagreed and tried to tell him that what he accomplished in life took a tremendous amount of courage and tenacity, and the proof was in the results of the family he reared. All of them learned to love, honor, and cherish each other and to accept each person for the goodness that they possess.

Joe's response to me was "That's nonsense; all I did was show up."

We are talking about a man who found more pleasure in playing cards with all the children at the table than going out to dinner or to a movie or dancing. All he did was "show up"! If that is the case, then I strongly suggest that we all learn how to "just show up." Instead, we are in a world where it is more important to be on late-night TV than to be where your responsibilities exist; where people who are paid to entertain us decide it is more important to tell us what we should believe and how we should think; where academic teachers will chastise and fail you if you don't think as they do. Why can't we just accept people for who they are and understand that they may have a difference of opinion? That is a good thing. Look for the goodness in everyone, find something to do in life, and "just show up."

Now, just as important as showing up is doing something about it. Many times, we are put in positions where we just don't know what to do. In my late teens, I worked as a lifeguard for a township that had a community lake with six beaches. In New York State, you had to have Green Cross certification. In addition to Red Cross lifesaving, you needed to complete courses in first aid, very much like EMTs have today.

I was working at a beach on a hot summer afternoon when a young boy came up to me and said that his mother thought that she was in labor. When I went to the woman to discuss her situation, she explained that she went into the water to cool off a bit, sat on her blanket, and started to have contractions. As I fought with the idea that I might have to deliver a baby, she mentioned that she thought it was more of a reflex from being in the cool water than it was a case of real contractions. She was adamant that she did not want to alarm anyone, and she decided to just dry off, thinking the contractions would subside in time. After a while, she realized that the contractions were becoming more frequent, and she noticed that her bathing suit was not drying in the sun—her water had broken.

There is really nothing in the book that tells you what to do in this situation, but I realized that something had to be done. I suggested that the woman get into a comfortable position, leaning under a large tree. I asked some adults to assist me in not making this a spectacle and to help me disperse the spectators. I also asked someone to call an ambulance to the beach and explain that there was the possibility of a birth.

I asked the woman if I could examine her to ascertain how far along the baby had come. After removing the bottom of her bathing suit, I saw a little patch of hair and explained that I thought the baby was crowning. From that point on, I had no idea what to do and what to expect. I was a deer in headlights. I decided that the best course of action would be to let nature take its course and suggested that the woman not do any pushing until we got further along.

In about fifteen minutes, the ambulance showed up with a doctor, and we transported her from the beach to the vehicle. The doctor told me to come along because he might need some help. I temporarily shut down the beach, entered the ambulance, and did exactly what the doctor told me to do. The hospital was a little less than five miles away, and the baby was born on the way. The doctor did all the work of delivering while I assisted in comforting the woman and assuring that she stayed in the correct position for delivery. When it was over, the doctor and the hospital staff commended me for my participation, at which time I said that I really didn't do anything. I later found out that by talking to the woman and comforting her through the delivery, I had helped immensely. Even better, the woman said I seemed to know what I was doing. I thought I had just showed up.

We are all put into positions of urgency that need to be acted upon. When these occur, not doing anything is not an option. Evaluate the situation, determine a course of action, stay calm, and act accordingly. When possible, solicit help. Consider what you might want done if you were the person needing help. Stay positive and do the very best you can. I think you will find that things have a way of working out.

So we discussed showing up and doing something. What's next? It's not just enough to show up, and it's not just enough to do something. It's a matter of how we show up and how we do something. Whatever we do, wherever we go, whomever we meet—leave what, where, and whom in a better position than when we arrived.

When I was a Boy Scout, I was taught that when you set up a campsite, you needed to leave that location in a better state than what it was when you first got there. Before doing anything, you needed to consider where you were going to set up your tents, your latrines, and your campfires. When you left, there should be no trace that a campsite was set up. This causes us to think before we act. We should do this with people, places, and activities.

My father, an Eagle Scout, made sure that this thought process was not just for campsites but in anything we would encounter. He would ask us questions from grade school to college and beyond: Did we leave a better school? Did we engage in extracurricular activities, including sports, clubs, and service projects? Did we do the best we could concerning grades? Did we help others in need and, by our example, show others that we cared? After graduation, were we model citizens who gave a good name to our schools? In our chosen jobs, did we have and share a commitment to doing things right? If we rented an apartment and moved, was it in better shape than when we moved in? If we purchased a house, did we enhance the landscaping, strengthen the structure inside and out, and when we moved, was it a better house than when we moved in? For people, places, and projects, strive to make the world a better place to live in. All it takes is some thought, planning, and follow through.

One more thing about showing up. Allow me to share with you a story. In September 1991, our region was woefully behind our annual objectives. At a cabinet meeting, I was embarrassed to say that I really couldn't put my finger on why we were lingering as a sales team. I called a meeting of my five regional sales managers to ascertain the reasons we were so far behind and what could be done to rectify the problem. These regional sales managers were responsible for forty direct-report district sales managers who were managing 703 agents throughout the state, along with over 1,500 associate producers. If we didn't do something quickly, we would never be able to make up the ground needed to attain objectives. At the meeting, the five regional sales managers were as perplexed as I was for our lack of performance. It wasn't a matter of talent, nor was it a matter of activity. The message was clear, but we weren't seeing results. We decided to bring in the entire sales-management team within the next few weeks to determine what was needed to be done to reverse this trend.

In October of that year, we met as a group and discussed our situation. Similar to the regional managers, no one could really put a finger on the reason for the results, and after two hours of discussion, we took a break. During that recess, I overheard many managers mention that the activity was adequate but the results were not appearing as fast as they thought they should. When we reconvened, I shared a story that I had heard some years before. It went like this:

Legend has it that three horsemen were traveling through the desert. From the earliest of times, we know that the desert has tested people's souls. After a long, hot day's journey, the three horsemen rested for the evening near a dried-up riverbed. They unsaddled their horses, ate some provisions, and readied themselves for an evening of sleep. As they laid their hands upon their saddles and gazed into the desert sky, they each heard a voice telling them to go down to the riverbed and grab some pebbles and put them in their saddlebag pockets. The first horseman said he wasn't interested in pebbles. The second horseman said he was too tired and would do it in the morning. The third horseman promptly acted and put a handful of pebbles into a pocket. That night, there was magic in the air. When the men awoke, the third horseman found that his pebbles had turned into diamonds. The first horseman was not interested and did not reap any benefits. The second horseman, a procrastinator, lost an opportunity and did not reap any benefits. The third horseman was both sad and glad—glad that he took the pebbles that turned into diamonds and sad that he did not take more.

Which type of person are you—the one who doesn't care, the procrastinator, or the person who takes action?

I concluded the meeting by explaining to the managers that the person who didn't care and the person who was the procrastinator achieved the same thing: nothing. I went on to further explain that if, in fact, managers were procrastinators, we didn't need them. In my opinion, there is no room for procrastination from a manager and that if they would use that as an excuse, they were really telling me they didn't care. I also went on to highlight that the third horseman was troubled that he did not seize the full opportunity. We agreed as a group that each and every one of us in that room was going to take an extra special look at how they were conducting their business affairs and, for the rest of the year, put their best foot forward, decisively, and seize the opportunity.

We ended our year exceeding all regional objectives and achieved Region of the Year.

CHAPTER 14

TIDBITS AND THANK-YOU NOTES

FOLLOW YOUR HEART, then your gut. Always keep your heart open in everything you do, and then when you get that gut feeling, follow it. If you don't, you may deal with constant regret. Remember, it's not the decision you make that will determine if it was a good decision. Often, it's what you do after you make the decision that will dictate whether it was a good or bad decision. If your heart is in it, most of the time, you've made the right decision.

Never ask something of someone else that you have never done or are unwilling to do yourself. Never give up on a worthy goal. The minute you do, you lose an opportunity.

There are really only two things that people want from the day they are born until the day they die: to be loved and to feel important. If you recognize that this applies in your daily activities, people will be attracted to you.

Understand that how you show up can affect your message. What you wear can speak much louder than what you say. However, you can use it to your advantage. When I was in the home office, we had quarterly marketing meetings. It was an opportunity to communicate to the entire marketing organization what the specific departments were doing. Senior leadership was in attendance, including, on occasion, the president of the company.

Before one such meeting, I was asked by our vice presidents to make a presentation on what we were doing with respect to new marketing initiatives that needed to be tested and approved. Our team agreed that what I was being asked to do was something we were not ready for and that I should not present. However, the request came from two executive vice presidents, and there would be no getting out of the presentation. I was advised to say something—but not too much—and I was not allowed to be evasive. The meeting was in two days. It was well known that I was of Italian descent and originally from New York City. I decided to use it to my advantage. When I entered the auditorium, I stood in the back of the room where only my department associates could see me. I was dressed in a white three-piece suit with a black tie and white shoes. When introduced, I walked down the aisle, the entire length of that auditorium, past the president and senior leadership. After some fun-loving comments and crowd laughter, I proceeded with a lighthearted presentation. The dissertation was over in fifteen minutes, and I concluded with the audience standing, clapping, and laughing. To this day, not one person heard or remembered what I had to say but only what I was wearing. Remember, what you wear can speak much louder than what you want to say.

I don't believe in coincidences. I don't believe in fate. I do believe in destiny, and because we have free will, I believe each and every person has within them the power to fashion their own destiny. We are all a product of our experiences, and events in our lives determine future experiences and behavior. Education is important, so is street-smart common sense. An only child has a different learning curve than a child with siblings. A person born in a position of wealth is in no better shape than a person reared in a lesser position of wealth.

The lessons learned and accepted by each bring them to the same place—that is, to have a keen awareness of where you are, what you have done, and how you are going to act. Then, and only then, will a person realize that he or she controls what happens next. It's not that we have all the answers now or, for that matter, know all the questions. It's a self-realization that how we react and act very much determines what is most important as we continue our life's journey. Think of the last time you thought something was coincidental. Now, reflect upon what brought you to that specific event. I suggest that your prior experiences and actions took you to that place and time—where it was not coincidental but predictable. Therefore, decide what impact you want on your future, and then go after it with all the fervor and sinew you can muster. That's the winning ticket.

The difference between successful and unsuccessful people is that successful people are willing to do what unsuccessful people are not willing to do. This includes interest, attitude, study, application, and effort. In addition, the difference between highly successful people and those who experience moderate success is about 2 percent to 3 percent extra effort. That extra effort comes in many ways. It could be time management, a better attitude, a heightened interest, or a constant smile on your face. In any event, this slight edge is what differentiates the best versus the mediocre.

If you can conceive, then believe you can achieve! Creativity. Imagination. Initiative. Ingenuity. Try it; you might like it.

Imagine your life as a powerful, free-flowing river. You alone determine the direction and strength of the river. If you allow clean mountain streams to enter your river, your life flow becomes more powerful with more direction. If you allow pollution and garbage to enter, your life flow becomes weaker with less direction, and it may get to the point where you do not survive. Amazingly, the choice is yours.

Accept change as an opportunity, not a challenge. In a constantly changing world, we tend to lose sight of the opportunities because we spend needless time worrying about the challenges. Like the saying goes, instead of asking "Why?" ask "Why not?"

SPECIAL THANK-YOUS

THE FORMATIVE YEARS

Thank you to *all* my immediate family—Mom, Dad, Richard, Michael, and Donna—for everything! To all my aunts, uncles, and cousins, for actively allowing me to grow in their space. To Grandpa Ignatius and Grandmas Louise and Cornelia, for constantly challenging me to be a better person. And to Nauna Petronella, for rocking me for hours on end to ease my colic.

THE SCHOOL YEARS

Thank you to all the Dominican Sisters at Saint James the Apostle, for teaching me the disciplines of learning, especially Sister Raymond Mary, for getting me ready for high school. To all the priests and lay teachers at Archbishop Stepinac High School, for teaching me time management and energy management, especially Father McCaffrey for suggesting the rifle team as a way to control my emotions. To all the Jesuits and professors at John Carroll University, for their Socratic method of teaching, enabling me to question, conclude, defend, and reference, especially Rev. Casey Bukala for starting me on my journey. He spent his entire life studying and defending existentialism and was the best philosophy teacher I ever met. To all my coaches, especially Gerry B.—the best coach I ever had, bar none—for seeing in me a talent that no one else recognized.

THE POST-COLLEGE YEARS

Thank you to all my friends, teammates, and confidants, for allowing me to experience life and grow at my own pace, especially Ricky, for not allowing me to get distracted from what's really important. Of course, my parents were always right there, but Ricky was a valued friend who validated what my parents taught me. To all the women who said yes to a date, for understanding my social awkwardness and being patient with me in learning about female friendship. Thank you, Dan, for making sure that my putter remains level and not pointed in; thank you, Skibo, for reminding me that I can't finish my swing at two o'clock; thank you, Rich, for suggesting that I change my golf ball to one more conducive for my desired flight; and thank you, again, to Dan, for teaching me to make good decisions in different scenarios.

THE WORKING YEARS

Thank you to all my clients, for helping me get on the road to success. To all my managers, especially Vinny M., for teaching me a better way; Paul M., for challenging me to consider management; Harry W., for taking me under his wing as I started my management career; Bill M., for pushing me to my limits in understanding corporate; Dimon M. and Phil L., for allowing me to take on an opportunity that no one else wanted and, in doing so, putting a fire in my belly that motivated me for years; Joe M., for keeping me sane when it seemed that everyone else was nuts; and Maggie, for saying yes and standing by me through all the challenges that come with the territory. To all my agents, for accepting me for who I was and agreeing to allow me to move them in the right direction—especially, in Rochester, Mark G., Dwane W., and especially Sharon C., my first female hire and proof that women can function in this industry better than anyone else thought at the time; in Philly, Jim B., Jim Y., Tom L., Rick H., Charlie M., Marshall A., Larry and Bobby C., Larry W., Rocco B.; in Harrisburg, Sonny L., John F., and special thanks to Rick L.; and, in Pittsburgh, Bobby M., Steve V., Tom F., and Scott G.; in Northern Virginia, to everyone for allowing me to wrap my arms around their agencies and, together, develop a game plan to accomplish things nobody thought possible, especially, Chris and Don, Leslie, Brent and Karin, Gregg, Amy, Chad and P. J., Mark H., Mark D., Laban and Josh, Matt and Chuck, Puff, and *all* their associate producers, too numerous to mention. And to all the managers who allowed me to supervise them, too numerous to mention.

THE MOST RECENT YEARS

Thank you to Phil S., for sharing Ann in a business capacity. To Ann, my work spouse, for talking with me every working day, motivating each other, and mostly, talking each other "off the bridge." To Terry S., for always being willing to listen and to discuss alternatives. Special thanks to Dave and Jan T., for convincing me to return, and to Mark B., who relit a fire inside me that had long burned out. Finally, to the golfers who play a major role in my recreational activities, especially Skibo, for teaching me how to relate to the group, J. D., Mark S., Pete T., Keith and Jim H., Bill W., Dan T., Rich M., and the rest of the slacks and townies. To George L., Dennis K., Kent, Orval, and the rest of the "retired men," for showing that you can still be competitive after age seventy and for keeping things exciting and fun.

LAST BUT NOT LEAST

Thank you to Maggie, my partner, for all the love she showed to me, for Nicholas and Rose, for all the support she gave me in the good times and the bad, for the caring and nurturing of our children, for the patience she had when things were going crazy, and for the courage to let me know when I was headed off the tracks.

To Nicholas, the first born, who, from the day he was born, made me realize that I could no longer take a cavalier approach in life because I was now responsible for another; for having great life goals and going after them with a zeal unmatched by most others; for teaching his sister through good example and developing a strong, loving relationship with her; and for staying strong with his faith-based beliefs.

To Rose, my daughter, for loving her family like no one else, for challenging me to challenge her, for having a commitment to excellence in all that she endeavored, for having a sense of humor to lighten discussions, for being heartfelt with all the people she encountered, and for being willing to take a risk when the reward could be great.

To all three, for buying into the priorities of God, family, and country/company and working hard in developing a strong family foundation where a great relationship was and is built.

www.ingramcontent.com/pod-product-compliance
Ingram Content Group UK Ltd.
Pitfield, Milton Keynes, MK11 3LW, UK
UKHW020416250726
13967UKWH00007B/2672